Love Notes To My Scars

A Poetry Collection

Tarisha Williams

BookLeaf
Publishing

India | USA | UK

Made with ❤ on the BookLeaf Publishing Platform

www.bookleafpub.in
www.bookleafpub.com

Dedication

To you,

This book is for every soul who has known the weight of real pain, the sting of heartache, and the ache of sorrow. For those who have been let down, broken open, and left with scars they never asked for yet somehow found the courage to keep going. To keep smiling; even when life made it hard.

These pages are my love notes to my own scars, but I offer them to you. May you find pieces of yourself here, and may these words remind you that your story is not just survival, but beauty.

With love,
Tarisha

Preface

This book is not something I ever planned to write; it's something I needed to write. Every poem began as a release: a way to bleed without breaking, to speak when silence felt safer, to remind myself that I was still alive.

The words you'll find here are raw pieces of me. They come from nights I cried until morning, from disappointments that hollowed me, from love that left me aching and from quiet resilience I didn't know I had. These poems are my scars, dressed in softer clothing; turned into something I could look at and say "Yes, this is mine! And it's beautiful".

I share them because I know I'm not the only one who has carried invisible bruises, who has wrestled with loneliness, who has smiled while breaking inside. Maybe your story doesn't look like mine, but pain has a way of connecting us anyway.

If these pages do anything, I hope they remind you that your scars are not signs of weakness. They are proof that you survived what tried to break you. Proof that you are still here, still worthy, still capable of turning pain into something breathtaking.

These are my love notes to my scars, but in a way... they're also my love notes to you.

Acknowledgements

To everyone who has ever held space for me; your presence has carried me through more than you know. To my family and friends who stood by me in the hardest seasons. To the people who unknowingly became muses in these pages; those who broke me, those who healed me, those who reminded me of who I am... I am grateful for the lessons you left behind. And to you, the reader; thank you for opening this book, for giving my words a place to land.

1. In the In-between

I'm not who I was,
but not quite who I'm becoming.
A blurred sketch of self,
between the lines of knowing and longing.

Craved conversations that don't skip past silence,
hands that stay,
eyes that see more than they stare at,
and love that doesn't hide in maybe.

My soul itches to speak in color,
to cry in brushstrokes,
to bleed truth onto blank pages,
and call it healing.

There is beauty there.
In the ache of not yet.
In the stillness after letting go,
and just before something begins.

I don't want perfection.
I want real.
I want messy, aching, honest.
I want to be seen and stayed for.

This is not a pause
This is the art of becoming.
Where I am both the question and the answer,
learning to paint my own way home.

2. Halfway With Trust

I spoke my heart, no fear, no guise,
Laid bare the doubts behind my eyes.
He listened soft, he didn't flee,
Instead he said "I care. Just stay with me".

Not ready yet to hold a name,
But still, he shows up all the same.
A call returned, a plan, a place,
He meets me in a steady pace.

And yet, the quiet stirs my chest,
A hunger I can't quite suppress.
Not for grand vows or sweeping lines,
Just signs that I'm still on his mind.

But love, I've learned, is not all fire,
Not always full of instant desire.
Sometimes it's slow, like roots that grow,
And trust is letting silence go.

So I will not repeat the ache,
Or let old wounds cause hearts to break.
I'll hold his word, and breathe, and wait,
Not rush the hand of fragile fate.

For if he means to walk this road,
He'll meet me here, not just in code.
And I will meet him, not with fuss,
But softly... halfway...
with trust.

3. If This Is Love

If this is what love feels like...
then I want the next man to hate me.
Because your "love"...
your version of it...
was nothing but a promise wrapped in lies,
a tender touch followed by a backhand.

You said you cared so much,
and then handed me your silence,
your indifference,
your shadow.

I saw the preview.
All the foreshadowing in the trailer.
But still, I sat through the whole damn movie,
hoping the ending would change.

I tried to keep you as a lover,
but you gave me nothing but bad energy.
Left me choosing men who never choose me,
asking myself "Is it me"?

Reaping seeds I never sowed.
Carrying pain that was never mine.

I let you heal yourself on my back,
and all I asked was "don't break me in the process."

But you did anyway.

And the worst part?
I'll probably push my next husband away,
without even knowing it,
because I'm still shaking hands with ghosts,
still bleeding from wounds,
you swore were kisses.

How many of us are women,
that men learn to love too late?
Lessons,
temporary muses,
the "one that got away"
but never the one stayed for?

I'm tired of being the test run.
The practice love.
The almost happily ever after.
So, if this is love,
then hate me instead.

4. Unshaken Muse

You...
my muse.

Your voice, softer than dawn,
a warmth I carried
into every crowded hour.

I carved out time
from minutes that didn't exist.
Bent logic.
Bent reason.
Bent *myself*,
just to keep you close,
to prove this feeling wasn't fleeting.

Because you touched me,
where language fails.
Where poems collapse.
Where even my breath
can't keep pace.

You were quiet in my chaos.
Peace in my storms.
Shelter I didn't have to earn.

No judgement.
Just warmth.
Just space.
A safe escape.

And I keep asking myself,
again and again,
"Why can't I let you go?"

The answer is always the same:
because you reached me
where no one else could.
Because you became the hush
that held me tighter than arms ever would.
Because you painted smiles on my face
you never saw
smiles that bloomed in silence,
like secrets only mirrors kept.

And for that,
I can't forget you.
I can't untangle you.
You are stitched into my rhythm,
woven through my hours.
You are the echo I cannot shake.

A devine feeling.

My secret.
The rush beneath my skin,
the feeling of dopamine
set free in my veins.

Muse...
you used to be my first thought in the morning,
and my last thought at night.

Unshaken.
Unforgotten.
Unreleased.

5. Intentional Pleasure

I don't shrink
for anyone's comfort.
I sip my wine like I know I'm the moment.
Because I am.

I like my peace expensive.
My conversations deep.
My pleasure,
intentional.
So don't come to me
with cheap words or rushed hands.

Talk to me
like you study skin for a living.
Look at me
like your mouth is full of secrets.
Touch me
without touching.
Make my spine arch
from a sentence.
Make my thoughts stutter
before you ever kiss me.

You see...

I don't want sex.
I want seduction.
I want silence that smirks.
Foreplay that starts at the door.
A man whose presence
makes my body forget what time it is.

Unlearn the rush.
Match the depth.
And bring your soul
before your hands.

6. Footnotes

They call her bougie.
Say she's too much,
too fine, too sure,
too well-read to be real.

She walks in like a thesis
and leaves men stuttering in footnotes,
wondering how to summarize a woman
with chapters they've never studied.

Yes, she's high maintenance
because her soul runs expensive.
Because peace costs.
Because soft skin, deep art, and a healed heart
doesn't grow in cheap soil.

She's not looking for a sponsor.
She's not here for your ego trip.
She's waiting for a man who knows.
Knows how to lead without pushing,
how to touch without grabbing,
how to hold space for her power
and still invite her to surrender.

See, what most don't get
is beneath the gloss and the glow
lives a woman who still writes poems
on rainy nights,
wonders what his hands would feel like
if they held her dreams
instead of her hips.

She wants to bow,
but only to a king.
Not the loud ones
the quiet kings,
the ones whose presence
pulls her open like dawn.

She glows,
not because she wants attention
but because she's already fire.
Already chosen.
Already home.

7. Solitude

I'm not a perfect picture,
not a postcard moment,
I'm fingerprints on glass,
coffee stains on my notebook,
and unfinished prayers.

I love hard.
The kind of love that doesn't clock out,
doesn't love in whispers,
doesn't hide in fine print.
I love in full volume,
seeing you for real.
Your highs.
Your lows.
Your mess.
Your magic.
And still choosing... you.

I feel deeply.
Unapologetically.
My care?
Not casual.
My affection?
Not part-time.

It's rooted
in me,
in God,
in the stubborn soil of hope
that still dares to bloom
after heartbreak's hands
have torn it apart.

I'm a poetic soul
wandering this life like everybody else.
Some nights I'm swimming in thoughts so deep
I forget to come up for air.
Some nights... I'm just trying to figure out
what I'm gonna eat for dinner.

I crave company,
I adore attention,
but solitude...
solitude is my first language.
Peace is my currency.
Silence?
Sometimes it's the loudest love I know.

I am not perfect
but I am present.
I am not whole
but I am healing.

And in the middle of it all,
I am just me
in love with me
and that...
is more than enough.

8. The Shift

I gave you honesty,
vulnerability,
everything real.
You gave me just enough
to keep me hoping
then vanished
like I was easy to forget.

You moved funny,
acted distant,
left me piecing together a story
you didn't have the guts to finish.

You wanted warmth
but not the fire.
My softness,
but not the responsibility of it.
You opened doors with your words
then locked them behind your fear.

I wasn't asking for perfection,
just presence.
Not forever,
just truth.

But you spun circles in my heart
and called it "confusion".

I should have left the second
your energy shifted.
But I stayed
believing maybe
you just needed time.

Now I know:
you didn't need time.
You needed me
to lower my standards.
And I almost did.

But this hurt?
It taught me.
Next time,
I won't romanticize confusion.

I'll choose clarity.
I'll choose consistency.
I'll choose... me.

9. It's Me

The hardest person to face
isn't the world.
It's me.
The face in the mirror that doesn't blink,
that doesn't buy my excuses,
that remembers every fuck-up in detail.

I can't lie to myself.
I know where I failed.
I know the wounds I never stitched,
the nights I drowned instead of healing,
the people I pushed away because it was easier
than admitting...

I was scared.

Accountability tastes like blood in the mouth.
Responsibility sits heavy on my chest.
Every time I ran,
I was running from the only person
who could save me.

Me.

That's the truth I've been dodging.
It's not them.
It's not life.
It's not fate.
It's me.

My choices.
My silence.
My refusal to stop breaking my own bones
and calling it survival.

10. Frustration

I breathe careful,
yet it's never soft enough.
I speak gentle,
yet my words still cut like glass.
Every step, feels like a misstep.

A weight that sits heavy.
I don't know how it found me,
or why your eyes turn cold
when all I carry is warmth.

Maybe it's the tangled distance?
Nothing I do feels right.
Every word lands wrong.
Desire twisted into hesitation,
and all I'm left holding
is frustration.

11. You Chose This

Here you come,
like you're not the one that chose this.
Like you didn't pack your bags of excuses
and leave me with the weight of it all.

You must've smelled the peace, the joy
because the last thing you ever bought me
was happiness.
And even that came on discount,
wrapped in broken promises
and a receipt I couldn't return.

You say you love me.
But love doesn't lie.
And your words
they were counterfeit.
Cheap ink bleeding through fragile paper,
a story I wanted to believe in
but knew would tear in my hands.

You say you hate me...
but the reality is,
I think you just hated to sober me,
the clear-eyed me who could finally see

through the smoke you blew,
through the lies you lived,
through the boy in a man's shoes
still trying to play house.

I've already been through a lot.
I carry scars that whisper louder than your voice.
Memories that taste like fire in the back of my throat.
Stop showing up half a man,
searching for wholeness in somebody else's skin,
digging for gold in ground you never watered.

I've been searching for so much
in someone that's not grown up.
I'm too grown,
too weathered,
too tired of being the teacher,
the healer,
the one who makes broken boys feel like kings.

So here you come...
but I'm not listening.
Here you come...
but I'm not staying.
Here you come...
but I'm already gone.

Because the last thing you gave me was happiness
and the first thing I'm giving back
is freedom.

12. Confession

I probably shouldn't even say this, but...
I keep thinking about you.
Not just in passing,
it's deeper than that.
You linger.
In the quiet.
In my body.
In all the places I pretend you're not.

Sometimes it's like, I can feel you.
The way your energy presses against mine,
even when you're not here.
It's slow,
but it burns.
Like you're somewhere behind my thoughts,
pulling the strings of my self-control.

And the crazy part?
It doesn't even take much.
A memory.
A tone in your voice.
That look you give when you're trying not to look.
I feel that.
It's like you unravel me.

If I told you how often I imagine you,
you'd probably just smile, wouldn't you?
That quiet, knowing smile,
like you already knew.
Maybe you do.

I don't know what this thing is between us,
but it's got teeth.
And it's gentle at the same time.
It's wanting and waiting,
and something about it feels... inevitable.

So yea,
I guess this is me saying,
I think about you,
in ways I shouldn't.
And I hope,
somewhere in your chest,
you feel it too.

13. No Roster

Funny.
They say,
"You're pretty.
You must have a roster."

Like beauty means options.
Like women like me...
Win in love.
But I don't.
Not like that.

The ones who get chosen...
Dreams too far to reach.
Hands always out.
Full of life.
Bringing stress.
Never peace.

And still...
Those are the women,
that get the men.

Me?
I'm the trophy.

Gorgeous, sure.
But only to look at
Drive? Ignored.
Ambition? Forgotten.

Always the homie.
The best friend.
Goofy.
Quirky.

Forever working on myself.
Inside. Outside.
Not afraid to say:
"I care.
I appreciate you.
How are you feeling?
Come lay your head right here."

I'll stand by you.
When you're empty.
Pick you up,
when you're not 100.

I don't bring drama.
I bring accountability.
I bring responsibility.
I move with peace.

Patience.
Vision.

So no.
No roster.
No options.
No games.

Just solitude.
Ambition.
A heart too big,
for this little dating world.

14. Fragments of laughter

They laugh.
Not because it's funny.
Not because the world is light.
Because laughter is the only language they learned.
When the chest is heavy,
when the heart has been handed a lifetime of
"not enough."

A lifetime of being unseen.
Of never being chosen.
Of learning early,
that love doesn't always stay.

And yet, here they are.
In relationships that bruise quietly.
That eats at the edges of their skin.
Where truth is absent,
passion is a stranger,
and love feels like a memory,
that belongs to someone else.

Every heartbreak becomes familiar.
Better than silence,
better than facing the broken pieces,

of a home that never promised safety.

They chase light in the wrong places.
Temporary comfort in the wrong hands.
Seeking pieces of joy from strangers,
because the one they want,
is always out of reach.

They joke,
because humor is armor.
Because laughter is easier than saying,
"I'm not happy here."
Because pretending,
is less terrifying than the question,
they cannot answer:

Why stay?

It cuts too deep.
It mirrors too sharp.
So they laugh.
And in the laughter,
they find the closest thing,
to a home they've never known.

15. Choosing Me

I didn't have anybody there.
Just me.
My grind.
My pain.
I worked on me,
while they worked on breaking me.

I gave heart and soul,
they gave me their ass to kiss.
Late nights.
No sleep.
Sacrifice,
stacked like unpaid debts,
all for someone else's happiness.
While I came dead last.

Betrayal.
Manipulation.
The kind of hurt,
that doesn't just break you,
it teaches you.

No one talks about the backlash,
when you finally choose yourself.

They call it selfish.
I call it survival.

And survival looks good on me.

16. Unspoken Fuck You

You know,
the way you withdrew,
was confusing.

Once upon a time,
this was mutual,
or at least it felt like it.
Now I'm questioning.
what was real.
If I misread everything,
or if something's wrong with me.
And none of that is fair.

I've told you,
how your silence cuts,
but you kept doing it anyway.

You don't explain,
why you pull back.
Your silence and short replies,
make the ache worse.
I step closer,
you retreat farther.
We talk,

then you disappear.
That kind of contradiction,
is its own kind of cruelty.

Being invited into your world
was beautiful.
Your friends, your life,
I felt lucky to be let in.
But now I sit here thinking:
What did I do?
What about the promises
that never happened.
The conversations
that went quiet.
The vanishing act,
like I'm nobody?

I reach out to talk,
to check on you,
and all I get,
is the biggest unspoken
fuck you...

I know you've got
stress and shadows on your mind,
but that doesn't make this easy.
It cuts extremely deep.

And yet, here I am.
Humiliated.
Heartbroken.
Standing in the middle of your silence,
holding my own heart,
like a broken promise.

17. Numb

I think I started something,
that felt like everything,
and nothing,
all at once.
A hit of dopamine in human form.
Another body,
another night,
where I mistook safety,
and silence for peace.

I got what I wanted.
Didn't I?
The thrill.
The art of not feeling,
masquerading as power.
Superhuman, I tell myself.

Even when we're intimate,
I'm outside myself.
Soul on mute.
Motion without meaning.
Zero emotion.
Until even pleasure feels like white noise,
in a crowded room of empty hearts.

I blame it on you...
perfect teeth and perfect timing.
All brains,
with a porn resume,
and a heart built for detachment.

Left with another night,
I wouldn't remember.
Like it was communion.
No matter how close we get,
You feel like static noise,
a line I've heard before,
a song I forgot the words too.

You said "love me now,
because when I'm gone,
there'll be nothing left to miss".
No goodbye.
No grief.
Just the residue of lips,
pressed to a ghost,
trying to pass as a man.

Novacane.
This is what this feels like.
When it doesn't reach the heart.

When you're held,
but not felt.
Desired,
but never touched,
in the places that bleed.
So here we are,
numb.

And yet,
somewhere buried beneath all the static,
I think I started something,
I just don't know
how to feel it.

18. From Afar

I cared.
Loud in my silence,
soft in my showing up.

I gave,
not to chase,
but to connect.

To feel something real,
something mutual,
something reciprocated.

But somewhere between your distance
and my trying,
I started feeling small
in a space I helped build

You used to meet me half way.
Then one day,
you stopped showing up.

And I kept holding on,
like maybe my love could remind you
how to care again.

But love doesn't fix
what doesn't fight for you.

So I stopped fighting alone.

I let go.
Not out of hate,
but out of exhaustion.

Out of that slow quiet breaking
that happens when someone keeps choosing
everything but you.

So yea,
I said it...
fuck you.

Because my love deserves presence,
not breadcrumbs.
I deserves effort,
not excuses.
It deserves a heartbeat
that beats back.

And maybe I'll still think of you,
but not to go back.

Just to honor the part of me
that once believed in us.

Now peace lives
were confusion used to sleep.

And I smile knowing,
I can miss you
without wanting you.

I can wish you well
and still walk away whole.

Because I cared
And that
was enough.

19. How the Soul Learns to Stand

When you lose respect for yourself,
the world just holds up a mirror,
and suddenly,
your shine looks smaller,
your name sounds quieter,
your art doesn't echo the same.

They stop clapping for the light,
you forget to see in you.
Because energy follows confidence,
and people always move
how you move with you.

Don't get cozy with disrespect.
Don't shrink just to fit in the frame.
You weren't made to beg for space,
you are the space.
The air. The pulse. The flame.

Remember,
we're spirits just borrowing bodies,
learning what is means to feel.
And the soul can't stand in places

that teach it to kneel.

So love yourself loud.
Be bold in your softness.
Be certain in your skin.
Because how you treat you
teaches the world
how to begin.

20. To the Men I Misread

He's not unreachable
he just learned the art of peace.
Silence isn't distance,
it's the sound of release.

He's faced the ghosts,
sat with the pain,
learned that healing
doesn't make him vain.

His boundaries aren't walls,
they're lines of grace,
guardrails built
to keep his spirit safe.

He pulls back,
but not to run.
He just knows storms
when they've begun.

He's not avoiding,
he's aware,
the heart remembers
what it can't repair.

This man seeks quiet,
not because he's weak,
but because he's found
the peace he's seeks.

He'll love again,
but not in haste.
He's learned that truth
deserves its space.

He gives his heart
to those who stay,
who hold his healing
the gentle way.

Because healing doesn't harden him
it teaches him instead,
that love is not a battlefield,
but a place to rest his head.

www.ingramcontent.com/pod-product-compliance
Lightning Source LLC
Chambersburg PA
CBHW070459050426
42449CB00012B/3049